Most Po|

Colombian Recipes

Quick & Easy

A Cookbook of Essential Food Recipes from Colombia

By

Grace Barrington-Shaw

More books by Grace-Barrington-Shaw:

Disclaimer

All reasonable efforts have been made to provide accurate and error-free recipes within this book. These recipes are intended for use by persons possessing the appropriate technical skill, at their own discretion and risk. It is advisable that you take full note of the ingredients before mixing and use substitutes where necessary, to fit your dietary requirements.

Contents

Introduction

Within the geographical location of South America, Colombia is bordered by Panama, Brazil, Venezuela, Ecuador and Peru. The close proximity of these countries to Columbia have an influence on its cuisine, as well as the various regions within Columbia which also contribute their own particular culinary flairs. The main influences on Colombia's cuisine are from the indigenous population, Spain, Africa and to a lesser extent Arabia.

In addition to influence from other cultures, the wide variety of flora and fauna across the country adds to the diversity of the dishes across the six regions.

Despite the regional variation in cuisine, some common ingredients you will be sure to find in many dishes include rice, potato, maize, cassava, legumes, cereals as well as meats such as chicken, fish, pork, beef, goat and of course, seafood.

In this cookbook you will find classic recipes that incorporate these influences and ingredients, recipes aimed at capturing the essence of Colombia. Well-loved meals, tasty snacks and appetizers along with main course and breakfast dishes are included to give you a true sense of Colombian culture. Whether you are planning for breakfast, lunch, dinner or a special event, this selection of recipes will help you to create an impressive Colombian menu.

I am sure that you will enjoy the tastes and smells of Colombia as you embark on this sensory adventure in your kitchen!

1. Bandeja Paisa

Bandeja Paisa is a name that bears a twofold meaning. Bandeja is the Spanish word for platter and Paisa is the name of a region in northwest Colombia. True to the name, Bandeja Paisa is a generous serving of a variety of foods that have been artfully combined. This meal includes pork, white rice, beans, ground meat, plantains, fried eggs, sausage and more. It is served on a tray or a platter to accommodate the impressive combination. This recipe is a labour of love but the flavor and texture you will receive from the combination of ingredients is well worth the effort!

Serves 4 people

Ingredients

2 ¼ cups white rice

4 Arepas (see Arepa recipe in this book)

4 ripe plantain slices (from one whole plantain)

½ cup hogao (* see ingredients below)

4 cans pinto beans (retain water)

2 ½ avocados

1 pound pork belly

4 Chorizo sausages

4 eggs

1 pound beef

1 teaspoon garlic paste

1 teaspoon all-purpose seasoning

Salt and pepper, as desired

For Hogao

2 cups fresh chopped tomatoes

2 ½ tbsps vegetable oil

¼ tsp ground pepper

1 minced clove garlic

1 tsp cumin

½ tsp salt

1 C chopped scallions

Preparation

1. Cook the white rice in the usual way.

2. Make four arepas according to the recipe which follows on the next page.

3. Fry the sliced plantains in oil and set aside.

4. To make the Hogao, put the oil to heat up in a saucepan and add all the ingredients.

5. Allow them to cook on a medium heat for ten minutes with occasional stirring.

6. Turn the heat down to low then cook for a further ten minutes, stirring every now and again, until the mixture thickens. Adjust seasoning to preferred taste.

7. Place the beans along with the liquid into a pot along with the required amount of hogao and all-purpose seasoning.

8. Cook until thickened then turn off heat.

9. Cook the ground beef in two pints of water seasoned with garlic, ground black pepper and salt.

10. When cooked, drain the meat, add to a food processor and grind finely then set aside.

11. Cut the pork belly into four pieces and boil in water to which salt has been added, for a couple of minutes.

12. Remove, pat dry then fry in a small amount of oil and set aside.

13. Fry the eggs whole, one by one, then set aside.

14. Remove the skin of the avocado and cut it into four even slices and set aside.

15. Boil the sausages in a little water (or beer) then follow with frying in some oil.

16. Take all the prepared ingredients, except for the beans, and arrange them nicely on four platters.

17. Serve the beans in separate bowls to go with each platter.

Pairs well with – refajo or sweet beer

2. Arepas

This maize based staple is an everyday food in Colombia and also in Venezuela. It is eaten with a variety of accompaniments, making it versatile enough to be enjoyed as part of breakfast, lunch, at snack time or even as a starter for dinner. Arepas bear similarity to the gordita from Mexico and the pupusa from El Salvador.

Serves 3 to 4 people

Ingredients

1 C arepa flour

1 C crumbled ricotta cheese

8 ounces water

2 tbsps water

⅛ tsp salt

2 ounces vegetable oil

Preparation

1. Combine the flour, cheese and salt together in a bowl with the water until thoroughly mixed.

2. Leave for a minute or two until the dough begins to stiffen as the water is absorbed.

3. Take three tablespoons of dough and make a ball then flatten by pressing between the palms to about quarter inch thickness.

4. Smooth the sides to remove any cracks then place on a wax sheet. Continue until all the dough is used up.

5. Heat the oil in a non-stick or cast-iron pan on a medium heat until it begins to ripple.

6. Fry the arepas in batches until golden brown, flipping once. (Each batch will take about eight to ten minutes to complete).

7. Drain on absorbent paper towels then serve as desired.

Pairs well with – jam, cheese, meat fillings, avocado, eggs etc

3. Fritanga

This is another platter dish in which the main ingredients are quite often fried. While some of the ingredients vary from region to region, you will typically find included the patacones, pork belly, pork ribs, papa criolla and yuca fries.

Serves 4 to 6 people

Ingredients

3 lbs pork ribs or other part (cut into pieces)

8 oz oil (to fry)

2 lbs cooked chorizo (cut into pieces)

4 oz aliños sauce

Alinos sauce

1½ tsp sazon Goya with azafrin

½ tsp cumin

8 ounces water

3 chopped scallions

2 crushed cloves garlic

½ chopped red pepper

½ green pepper, chopped

½ chopped onion

Patacones (see recipe in this book)

Yuca fries

2 lbs fresh or frozen yuca (cassava)

Vegetable oil

½ tbsp salt

Papa criolla

2 lbs frozen papa criolla

½ tsp salt

4 tbsps olive oil

½ tsp black pepper

Other ingredients

1 large tomato, sliced into wedges

Guacamole

Aji

Lime wedges

Hogao

Preparation

To prepare the alinos sauce:

1. Put all the ingredients into a food processor or blender to make the paste.

2. Store in a glass jar, cover and keep refrigerated for one week.

To prepare the pork:

3. Season the ribs and pork meat with aliños sauce and refrigerate for a minimum of three hours or overnight, in a covered dish.

4. To cook, place the oil in a frying pan on a medium heat.

5. Add the meat to the hot oil and fry for fifteen minutes or longer if needed. They should be golden brown. Set aside.

To prepare the yuca fries:

6. Boil the yucca in a pot with salted water, cooking for a total of about twenty minutes.

7. Dry the pieces with a paper towel, then measuring half inch thickness slice into strips.

8. In a large skillet, heat the oil to 350 F then carefully add the yuca strips, frying to golden brown for about eight minutes on both sides.

9. Remove the yuca strips and drain. Season with salt.

To prepare the papas criollas:

10. Warm the oven on 400 F beforehand.

11. Combine the oil, pepper and salt in a large container then add the potatoes and coat them thoroughly.

12. Place the potatoes on a baking tray and bake for forty minutes or so.

13. Season with salt.

14. Prepare the patacones and set aside.

15. When all ingredients have been prepared, arrange them on a serving platter and add the tomato wedges, guacamole, hogao, lime wedges and aji.

Pairs well with - cold beer, guacamole, Colombian hot sauce - aji, lime wedges, hogao

4. Buñuelos

Buñuelos are a popular fried breakfast item and also popular at Christmas time. You will find the amounts of flour to cornstarch and the sweetness level, may vary across Colombia. The soft dough can be a little tricky for first time makers but they are super delicious once you have made it over that hurdle.

Serves 7 people

Ingredients

2½ C. Colombian quesito, grated

⅓ C cassava flour

1 large egg

2 tbsps milk

¼ C cornstarch

2 tbsps sugar

¼ tsp salt

1 tbsp baking powder

Vegetable oil

Preparation

1. To make the dough, leave the oil aside and place all the other ingredients in a bowl. Mix using your hands to create the dough.

2. Make small balls from the dough.

3. Place the oil into a deep pot and heat it up to 150°C.

4. Slowly drop the balls in one at a time and cover the pot for about four minutes.

5. Increase the heat slightly then fry them until they become golden brown in color.

6. When finished, allow them to drain on a paper towel then serve.

Pairs well with – hot chocolate, coffee

5. Colombian Empanadas

Empanadas are a type of stuffed fritter and are generally filled with shredded beef and pork but may also be made with ground meat instead. They are enjoyed as a snack in Columbia

This is the vegetarian version which uses potatoes as the filling, instead of meat.

Serves 4 to 5 people

Ingredients

Vegetable oil (to fry)

Lime wedges and ají, to serve

To Make Dough or Masa

1 ½ C yellow cornmeal, precooked

2 C water

1 tbsp vegetable oil

½ tbsp sazon Goya (with azafran)

½ tsp salt

Filling

2 C peeled white potatoes, diced

1 tbsp olive oil

¼ C white onions, chopped

½ lb pork and beef mix, ground

1 C tomatoes, chopped

½ tsp salt

¼ C green onions, chopped

1 garlic clove, chopped

2 tbsps fresh cilantro, chopped

1 bouillon cube

2 tbsps red bell pepper, chopped

¼ tsp black pepper

Preparation

1. To make the dough, put the pre-cooked cornmeal in a big bowl and add the sazon seasoning. Mix it well.

2. Pour in the water and oil, then mix to make the dough.

3. Make the dough into a ball then knead it for two minutes until it becomes smooth. Cover it with a dry, clean cloth and rest for twenty minutes.

To Make the Filling:

4. Cook the potatoes along with the bouillon cube in a pot of boiling water for about twenty-five minutes.

5. Drain, mash and set aside for later.

6. In a large pan, heat the olive oil and cook the onions for seven minutes, with frequent stirring.

7. Add to the same pan the tomatoes, garlic, bell peppers, green onions, cilantro, black pepper and salt. Continue to cook for a further twenty minutes.

8. Add in the pork and beef then cook while stirring for a further fifteen to twenty minutes, until most of the liquid has dried off.

9. Pour the meat into the container with the mashed potatoes and combine them well.

10. Separate the dough into a tablespoon and half-sized balls.

11. Roll the balls out very thinly between two pieces of plastic wrap to make a circle.

12. Remove the top layer of plastic and add a tablespoon of filling in the centre of each flat circle.

13. Use the plastic wrap to fold the dough into a semi-circle, then use the tines of a fork to seal the edges.

14. Pour the oil for frying in a large pot and let it heat up to 360 F on a medium heat.

15. Fry the empanadas three to four at a time, for about two minutes on each side until they are golden brown.

16. Allow them to drain on paper towels to remove the excess oil then serve.

Pairs well with – Aji and lime wedges

6. Patacones

Patacones, also called twice fried green plantains in other cultures, are a hugely popular dish. The plantains are sliced into rounds, fried, smashed then fried again. They make a nice side dish and also serve as a breakfast accompaniment.

Serves 2 to 3 people

Ingredients

2 green plantains, large

Oil for frying

Salt

Preparation

1. Remove the skin from the plantains then cut them into half inch-thick rounds.

2. Place the oil to heat in a heavy skillet on medium high.

3. Place some of the rounds into the oil and fry for three to four minutes on each side.

4. Remove and place on a paper towel then fry the rest.

5. Allow for about three minutes of cooling then smash each round between two layers of plastic wrap to about half the present thickness. You may use a jar or other flat object to smash them.

6. Make a salt water solution with the salt and dip the smashed plantains one by one into it. Take care when frying them the second time around since the oil may splatter from the water droplets.

7. Fry for another three minutes on each side then transfer to a paper towel to drain. Sprinkle a little more salt then serve while still hot.

Pairs well with – guacamole, tomato sauce, salsa, hogao, aji, fish dishes.

7. Sancocho

Sancocho is a soup dish which can include meat or pigeon peas. In addition, it includes plantains, Irish potatoes and yuca. Originally, it was made with hens as the protein component but as mentioned before other meats including fish may be substituted. It is also tradition to cook Sancocho on an outdoor fire which imparts a lovely smoky flavor, however it is also quite delicious when prepared on an indoor stovetop.

Serves 6 to 8 people

Ingredients

3 ears corn, cut into 3 pieces each

12 C water

4 ounces aliños

1 whole chicken, large

1 tsp salt

2 green plantains (remove skin and cut lengthwise into two pieces)

2 cubes chicken bouillon

6 medium-sized Irish potatoes (skin removed, cut in half)

1 lb frozen yuca (cut into large pieces)

¼ C fresh cilantro, chopped

¼ tsp ground pepper

Preparation

1. In a large pot add the chicken, completely cover with water, then add the chicken aliños, bouillon, salt, corn and green plantains

2. Allow to boil then turn heat down to a medium heat and continue to cook for half an hour.

3. Add the yuca, pepper and potatoes and cook for another half an hour until the vegetables are tender.

4. Add the cilantro, stir, taste, then season to desired taste. Enjoy.

Pairs well with – avocado, white rice and ají

8. Colombian Tamales

Tamales in Colombia are enjoyed around Christmas and New Year, but can also be eaten all year-round. It is one of the must try foods when you visit Colombia. While the filling tends to vary from region to region, it is common that the contents are wrapped in banana leaves or corn husks and the outer portion is made of Masa. To get an exceptionally flavorful tamale, the meat is marinated over night to develop flavor.

Serves 6 people

Ingredients

For Marinade

1 large chopped onion

4 cloves garlic

1 large chopped red bell pepper

1 large chopped green bell pepper

4 chopped scallions

4 tbsp ground cumin

3 tbsp sazon Goya with color

Salt

2 C water

For Filling

1 lb pork belly, divided into 12 cuts

1 ½ lbs pork, divided into 12 cuts

2 lbs pork ribs, cut into pieces with bones still in

3 large peeled and diced potatoes

1 C peas (may be fresh or frozen)

1 C peeled and diced carrots

For Masa

1 lb yellow masarepa (precooked corn meal)

5 C water

Salt

½ C marinade

2 tbsps sazon Goya (with color)

For Wrapping

2 lbs banana leaves (cut into 15-inch long pieces)

String to tie

Water and salt for cooking tamales

Preparation

1. Gather all of the ingredients to make the marinade and put them into a blender and blend until a smooth mixture is obtained. (Half a cup of the marinade will go toward making the masa).

2. Add a cup and a half of the marinade to the meat in a bowl and place it covered in the refrigerator overnight.

3. To make the masa, add the masarepa, water, sazon, salt and left-over marinade to a big bowl and mix with a wooden spoon or by hand.

4. Wash the banana leaves in hot water and place to dry.

5. To put the tamales together, put two leaves on top of each to make a cross, on a flat surface.

6. Take three quarters of a cup of the masa and spread it on the leaves in the centre.

7. Add one piece of each meat, a tablespoon of peas and carrots and two tablespoons of potatoes atop the meats.

8. Fold the leaves upward one side at a time to enclose the filling in the masa, overlapping the ends of the leaves, then tie with string. Follow suit for the remaining mixture.

9. In a large pot with boiling salted water, add the tamales and cook them, covered on a low heat for an hour and 45minutes.

10. When the tamales are cooked, remove them from the water and rest for five minutes before serving, using the leaves as a plate if desired.

Pairs well with - hogao

9. Cholado Colombiano

This lovely fruit salad has a wonderful medley of fruit and sweeteners and is the perfect summer cooler. It is also very appealing to the eye and is commonly sold at stalls in the street.

Serves 4 people

Ingredients

1 C bananas, chopped

1 C mangoes, chopped

1 C lulo

1 C papaya

1 C passion fruit

Strawberry syrup (or cordial)

5 C crushed ice

Sweetened condensed milk

Milo

Preparation

1. Place the crushed ice into two large cups then add a cup of syrup or cordial to each.

2. Add in some papaya and mango, followed by a heaping teaspoon of crushed ice and top with chopped bananas, lulo and passion fruit.

3. Drizzle some condensed milk over the fruit salad in each cup and add a sprinkling of milo if desired.

Pairs well with – wafers, shredded coconut

10. Churros

Churros are a crispy type of fried donut covered in sugar and cinnamon. They are quite quick to make and serve as a delicious snack. Be sure to have a star shaped tip for your piping bag to get the characteristic shape.

Serves 8 people

Ingredients

½ C water

½ C buttermilk

½ C butter

Pinch salt

1 tsp sugar

1 ¼ C flour

1 tsp vanilla

3 eggs, large

2-3 C vegetable oil (for frying)

½ C sugar

1 tsp cinnamon

Preparation

1. Place the buttermilk, salt, water, butter and a tablespoon of sugar into a saucepan on the stove and bring the contents to a boil.

2. Add in all the flour and continue to stir with a wooden spoon or spatula until the mixture forms a ball.

3. Cook for about two more minutes as you continue to turn the dough over in the pan, then remove from the hot burner.

4. One by one, add the eggs mixing after each is added, along with the vanilla. (The mixture will be a little stiff and shiny. If not shiny and too stiff, add another egg).

5. Add the mixture to a pastry bag with a star tip fitted. (Opening should be around half an inch. If you do not have a star tip a round one will do).

6. You may pipe four to six-inch pieces of dough onto wax paper or choose to pipe directly into the oil. If using the wax paper, place it on a cookie sheet and then place the churros into the freezer while the oil heats up to 375 F.

7. When the oil gets to the desired temperature, add the hardened churros batch by batch, frying for two minutes per side.

8. Place the golden-brown churros on a paper towel lined tray or plate to drain.

9. Make a half cup mixture of sugar with cinnamon, place it on a flat plate and roll the warm churros in the mixture to coat them.

Pairs well with – chocolate dip

11. Ajiaco

While some people regard this as a soup, it is also seen as a stew. Whatever the classification, ajiaco consists of chicken, potatoes and the herb guascas which imparts a distinct and pleasing flavor. It is great for cold weather or just as a comfort food.

Serves 6 to 8 people

Ingredients

4 Skinless chicken breasts

3 ears corn (each cut into two)

Pepper to desired taste

3 escallions *spring onions*

2 ½ minced garlic cloves

3 tbsps cilantro, chopped

2 C papa criolla

3 white potatoes (medium-sized, peeled and sliced)

3 red potatoes (medium-sized, peeled and sliced)

3 chicken bouillon cubes

1/3 C guascas *(Raw organic chocolate)*
substitute dried oregano

½ tsp salt

11 C water

Preparation

1. Put all the ingredients except the potatoes and guascas into a deep enough pot and allow to boil.

2. When the water begins to boil, continue cooking on medium heat for forty minutes. Remove chicken once cooked and set aside.

3. Cook for thirty minutes more then remove the scallions and add in the potatoes and guascas. Cook for an additional half an hour.

4. Add salt and pepper to taste then cut the chicken into small pieces and return to the pot. Serve hot.

Pairs well with – capers, heavy cream

12. Cazuela de Mariscos

This is a creamy and hearty stew which consists of two or more types of shellfish as well as fish, heavy cream and coconut milk. It is quite common in the coastal areas of Colombia and is a special occasion dish. You will find that shellfish is often used to make this dish without the addition of fish, this is purely preference. The addition of fish does increase the richness.

Serves 4 to 6 people

Ingredients

½ C green pepper, chopped

½ C red bell pepper, chopped

1 C onion, chopped

2 ½ garlic cloves, minced

1 C carrot, grated

1 fish bouillon cube

¼ tsp paprika

4 C heavy cream

13.5 ounces coconut milk (or 1 can)

1/3 C white wine

12 scrubbed littleneck clams

2 lbs jumbo shrimp (peeled and deveined)

2 lbs swordfish (1" pieces)

1 tbsp fresh cilantro, chopped

1tbsp fresh parsley, chopped

1tbsp tomato paste

1 tbsp butter

1 tbsp olive oil

Preparation

1. Place the butter and olive oil to warm in a saucepan on a medium heat.

2. Add the peppers, onion, garlic and carrots, then sauté for ten minutes until they become translucent.

3. Add the salt and pepper.

4. Pour in the cream and add the bouillon and coconut milk then allow to come to a boil.

5. Add all the seafood and with the pan covered cook on a low heat for two minutes to allow the clams to open.

6. Remove the pot from the heat and throw away any clams which remain unopened.

7. Add in the white wine and tomato paste and allow to simmer for about twenty minutes.

8. Use the cilantro and parsley as garnish then serve hot.

Pairs well with – white rice

13. Refajo

This cocktail is a mixture of beer and a specific brand of soda, Colombiano. It is similar to Shandy from the Caribbean and may vary slightly in flavor if aguardiente is added. Be sure to try this out at any Colombian restaurant.

Serves 6 to 8 people

Ingredients

1 L Colombiana Soda

2 L beer

4 C ice

3 aguardiente shots (if desired) *(substitute white Rum)*

Preparation

1. Combine all the ingredients together in a pitcher and serve.

Pairs well with – grilled meats, asados

14. Chocolate con Queso

This interesting combination of hot chocolate with cheese, a combination of salty and sweet, is popular during cold weather periods. It is enjoyed particularly at breakfast time but there is no rule against having it much later either.

Serves 2 people

Ingredients

1 L milk or water

6 tbsps chocolate powder

1 mozzarella ball

Preparation

1. Place the water or milk in a medium-sized saucepan and simmer on a medium heat.

2. Add the chocolate with constant stirring and turn the heat down when the liquid begins to bubble.

3. To serve, place half of the cheese at the bottom of two teacups and pour on the hot chocolate.

Pairs well with – bread, arepas

15. Tajadas de Plátano

Tajadas de Plátano are a commonly found side dish all over Colombia and are made from fried ripened plantains. It is a very simple dish to prepare and frying the plantains enhances their sweetness.

Serves 6 to 8 people

Ingredients

3 very ripe large plantains

4 ounces vegetable oil

Preparation

1. Remove the skin from the plantains and slice them into half-inch thick diagonal slices.

2. Fry them on a medium high heat in a large enough pan into which the oil has been heating up.

3. Fry the plantains in a single layer for about two minutes per side.

4. Place them to drain on paper towels then serve while still warm.

Pairs well with – shredded cheese

16. Arroz con Coco Titoté

This sweet rice cooked in coconut milk is also known as arroz con coco y pasas and is delicious with many accompanying meats. The Caribbean influence on this dish is clear from the use of coconut milk, which can be used from a can or freshly made.

Serves 4 to 6 people

Ingredients

2 C coconut milk

1 C long-grain rice

1 tsp salt

2 C water

2 tbsps sugar

1/3 C raisins

Preparation

1. Cook the coconut milk in a sauce pan for about half an hour on a medium heat. Stir regularly.

2. Add the rice and continue to stir. Cook for two minutes, then add the water, sugar, raisins and salt and allow it to boil. Stir only once at this point.

3. Turn the heat down to a simmer and cover. Rice is cooked once water has been absorbed.

4. Remove from the hot burner and rest for five minutes before serving.

Pairs well with – fried trout, stewed yuca

17. Pandebono

These savoury snacks are so simple to make and are great for people with gluten intolerance. They can be enjoyed at breakfast to give your day a nice warm start.

Makes 12 pandebonos

Ingredients

2/3 C Yuca flour

¼ C precooked masarepa or cornmeal

1 C Mexican queso fresco (Colombian quesito can be substituted)

1 ¼ C feta cheese

1 large egg

Preparation

1. Set the oven to 400 F.

2. Pace the flour, cornmeal and cheese in a food processor and combine, then slowly add the egg with the processor still running.

3. Make twelve equally shaped balls from the mixture then place on a lined baking tray.

4. Bake for fifteen to twenty minutes then serve warm.

Pairs well with – chocolate milk, butter

18. Bocadillo con Queso

This super simple dessert/appetizer requires no skill at all to prepare. It is simply guava paste with cheese slices, however they give an amazing flavor when combined. You may even experiment with other types of cheese, such as cream cheese, mozzarella and feta.

Ingredients

Guava paste, sliced

White cheese, sliced

Preparation

1. Arrange the guava paste and cheese slices on a plate or platter and you're all set.

Pairs well with – crackers, bread

19. Torta Negra

This cake is ever present at special occasions in Colombia. That means you are sure to find it all year round as birthdays, anniversaries and weddings call for torta negra. You will also find other variations of this recipe across the different regions of Colombia.

Serves 6 to 12 people

Ingredients

2 C pitted prunes

2 C raisins

1 C port wine

½ C dark rum

2 C candied figs

1 lb butter

1 lb sugar

1 dozen large eggs(room temperature)

1 lb all purpose flour

1 tsp baking powder

1 tsp ground cinnamon

½ tsp ground nutmeg

½ tsp ground cloves

1 tbsp vanilla extract

3 tbsps baker's caramel/molasses/dulce quemado

Preparation

1. Place the dried fruit to soak in a mixture of half cup of wine and a quarter cup of rum a week or two prior to making the cake. Use a glass container.

2. Set the oven to preheat at 350 F.

3. Grease and flour two eight inch cake pans.

4. Blend the soaked fruit with the liquid for about a minute then pour into a bowl.

5. In a separate bowl, combine the flour, baking powder, ground cinnamon, ground cloves and nutmeg.

6. In another container cream the butter and sugar using an electric mixer, then add the eggs several at a time as well as the vanilla.

7. Add the dry mixture to the creamed ingredients and continue mixing on a low speed for one minute.

8. Add the caramel and mix for another minute followed by addition of the fruit, using a wooden spoon to stir.

9. Split the batter equally between both floured pans then place in the oven and bake for roughly an hour and forty minutes. A knife inserted in the centre should come out clean when they are completely baked. Rest outside of the oven for at least ten minutes.

10. Remove the cakes from the pans and add top with the leftover wine and rum.

Helpful tip: To store, wrap the cakes in cling film followed by aluminium foil and leave for three days at room temperature before serving.

Pairs well with – vanilla ice cream, egg nog

20. Changua

This dish is certainly not typical as it is a soup which is traditionally served at breakfast time, although it can be enjoyed at any time of day. It is believed to be a good hangover cure for some. Bread is generally served in the soup or as a side.

Serves 4 people

Ingredients

4 C milk

2 C water

4 eggs

½ C fresh cilantro, chopped

3 scallions, chopped

Salt and pepper to taste

Preparation

1. Boil the milk and water then add the salt, pepper and scallions, cooking for three minutes.

2. Turn the heat down to medium then crack the eggs and add them whole, being careful not to break the yolks.

3. After three minutes of cooking, add the cilantro and serve.

Pairs well with – bread and butter

Conclusion

You will have found that some Colombian recipes reflect dishes that can be found in parts of the Caribbean, such as fried green or ripe plantains and the torta negra or black cake, however Colombia possesses many unique dishes that vary widely across the country. The Columbian tastes and aromas are unrivalled and the sensations are even greater when cooking these dishes for yourself and your loved ones. I hope you have enjoyed this classical taste of Colombia and that you will continue to excite your palette with these recipes.

Why not try one of my other Caribbean recipe books or simply create your own by using **My Caribbean Recipes Journal**, which contains blank recipe templated pages, ready for you to build a collection of your own!

Also, **visit www.ffdrecipes.com** to receive free exclusive access to our World Recipes Club, giving you FREE best-selling book offers and recipe ideas, delivered to your inbox regularly.

Cooking Measurements & Conversions

Oven Temperature Conversions

Use the below table as a guide to establishing the correct temperatures when cooking, however please be aware that oven types and models and location of your kitchen can have an influence on temperature also.

°F	°C	Gas Mark	Explanation
275°F	140°C	1	cool
300°F	150°C	2	
325°F	170°C	3	very moderate
350°F	180°C	4	moderate
375°F	190°C	5	
400°F	200°C	6	moderately hot
425°F	220°C	7	hot
450°F	230°C	8	
475°F	240°C	9	very hot

US to Metric Corresponding Measures

Metric	Imperial
3 teaspoons	1 tablespoon
1 tablespoon	1/16 cup
2 tablespoons	1/8 cup
2 tablespoons + 2 teaspoons	1/6 cup
4 tablespoons	1/4 cup
5 tablespoons + 1 teaspoon	1/3 cup
6 tablespoons	3/8 cup
8 tablespoons	1/2 cup
10 tablespoons + 2 teaspoons	2/3 cup
12 tablespoons	3/4 cup
16 tablespoons	1 cup
48 teaspoons	1 cup

8 fluid ounces (fl oz)	1 cup
1 pint	2 cups
1 quart	2 pints
1 quart	4 cups
1 gallon (gal)	4 quarts
1 cubic centimeter (cc)	1 milliliter (ml)
2.54 centimeters (cm)	1 inch (in)
1 pound (lb)	16 ounces (oz)

Liquid to Volume

Metric	Imperial
15ml	1 tbsp
55 ml	2 fl oz
75 ml	3 fl oz
150 ml	5 fl oz (¼ pint)
275 ml	10 fl oz (½ pint)
570 ml	1 pint
725 ml	1 ¼ pints
1 litre	1 ¾ pints
1.2 litres	2 pints
1.5 litres	2½ pints
2.25 litres	4 pints

Weight Conversion

Metric	Imperial
10 g	½ oz
20 g	¾ oz
25 g	1 oz
40 g	1½ oz
50 g	2 oz
60 g	2½ oz
75 g	3 oz
110 g	4 oz
125 g	4½ oz
150 g	5 oz
175 g	6 oz
200 g	7 oz
225 g	8 oz
250 g	9 oz
275 g	10 oz

350 g	12 oz
450 g	1 lb
700 g	1 lb 8 oz
900 g	2 lb
1.35 kg	3 lb

Cooking Abbreviations

Abbreviation	Description
tsp	teaspoon
Tbsp	tablespoon
c	cup
pt	pint
qt	quart
gal	gallon
wt	weight
oz	ounce
lb	pound
g	gram
kg	kilogram
vol	volume
ml	milliliter
fl oz	fluid ounce

Printed in Great Britain
by Amazon